DEDICATED TO:

Ryan Patrick Halligan, Jaheem Herrera, Jared High,
April Himes, Kasey Hone, Megan Meier, Joshua Melo,
Eric Mohat, Laura Rhodes, James Rogers, Daniel Scruggs,
Carl Joseph Walker-Hoover

3

ABOUT HEY U G L Y, INC.

Being a teenager isn't easy. It's difficult dealing with everything life throws at you - balancing school with your social life, meeting the expectations of your parents and wanting the approval of your friends ... it's exhausting! That's why we created Hey U G L Y, Inc.

Hey U G L Y was founded in 2002 in response to the daily headlines describing the increase in teen suicide, gun violence in schools, bullying, drug abuse, eating disorders, and the obesity epidemic facing American youth. In 2004 Hey U G L Y, Inc. became a 501(c)(3) nonprofit organization.

Our mission is to save the lives of teens and tweens by empowering them to deeply understand and embrace that they are U G L Y - *Unique, Gifted, Lovable ... and it's okay to be the You that they are.*

This Stop Bullying Handbook is a vital resource for helping you and your friends end bullying. If you are being bullied or know someone who is, this book will help you. Sometimes it's difficult for adults to understand the full impact of what you and your friends go through. This handbook was designed to give **YOU** a voice against bullying and the courage to **BE PART OF THE SOLUTION.**

Since Hey U G L Y's co-founder, Sporty King created the U G L Y acronym -

Unique Gifted Lovable You - the message has reached over 650,000 students through our in-school presentations, Website, radio show, Emotional Learning Activity Plans, contests and work with schools, community organizations, and youth development professionals. 650,000 is a lot but we have millions to go and you can help. This handbook will tell you how you can be a part of a worldwide movement to end bullying.

ACKNOWLEDGMENTS

FIRST and foremost to documentary filmmaker, Rick Erwin, my life partner, best friend, and collaborator.

To Chris Erwin who is a key inspiration for our programs, mission and determination to empower teens and tweens.

To Sporty King who created the acronym Hey U G L Y and continues to inspire all who are lucky to hear his inspirational messages.

Special thanks and gratitude to the educators and students who participated in this project: Dr. Sue Bryant, Principal and teacher Carrie Miller of St. Stanislaus Kosta School (St. Stans). Principal Greg Handel and Educational Advisor, Ingrid Voelker of La Porte High School. *Extra special thanks* to the founding members of **Hey U G L Y's student Stop Bullying Task Force from St. Stans:** Matt N., Scott S., Adrienne F., Olivia H., Sydney S., Skyler L., Alex M., Connor P., Tony P., Lindsey J., Silk H., Darria B., Elliott S., Alexcis O., Mikey R., Matt P., Maddy W. Appreciation to **Hey U G L Y's student Stop Bullying Task Force from La Porte High School**: Rachel C., Ben B., Julia G., Victor V., Trevor S., Hayley T., Courtney H., Carlos M., Ali H., Antonio F., Martin G., Brandi M., Simmie M., Vanessa M., David C., Jesus F., Kadie H.

To our sponsors: U S Banner Corporation, LaPorte High School, St. Stanislaus Kosta School, Marquette High School, Decal Arts & Signs, The LaPorte Herald Argus, Michigan City News Dispatch, Taco Bell®, Purdue University North Central, Klassman Financial Services, Kroger, GoHealthInsurance.com, Michigan City Community Enrichment Corporation, Kroczek's Lawn Landscape, Wrigley, Color House Graphics

To my dear friends and supporters: Dean Klassman, Judy Kroczek, Pam Nelson, Robert Swan, Barb Collins, Rieva Lesonsky, Gail Isaacson, Mike Cortson, Judy Jacobi, Sue Dabagia, Mary Ann Merrion, Sharon Dettmer, David Madison, Karen Raines, Theresa Blandin, Therese Luce, Dr. Jim Kestner, Ron Rosenblum, WRHC-FM, Daniel Gurfinkel, Radio Disney, Geoff Thursby, Brad Reisig, Patrick Kellar, Ron Berlotti

INTRODUCTION

THERE are lots of books written for adults and teachers about bullying – but this isn't one of them. This is for you, because **you're** the ones on the front lines. You know what happens when no one is looking.

Bullying is a serious issue. Approximately 864,000 teens report staying home from school one day a month because they fear for their safety.[1]

Our team at Hey U G L Y remembers what it was like to be bullied when we were your age. We even remember, and regret, the times we were the bullies. But that was then and this is now. Since we are no longer your age we wanted to know what happens when adults aren't looking so we began working directly with students to find out what's really going on. A national survey of students in grades 6-10, found 13 percent reported bullying others while 11 percent reported being the target of bullies. Experts say the facts are troubling, because bullying too often leads to violence, loss of self-esteem, depression and even suicide[2].

You can help stop it. This handbook was designed to let you have a voice about what is happening out there. Throughout this handbook you will be asked to email us with your thoughts and suggestions. Your input is important and we will be sharing it with students throughout the world. So you have the opportunity to help lots of kids across the globe.

Sometimes it's hard for adults to understand the full impact of what you and your friends go through. So pull together a group of your friends and get started on creating your **Hey U G L Y Stop Bullying Task Force**. Once you complete all of the chapters and exercises in this book, you and your group will become **OFFICIAL MEMBERS** of Hey U G L Y's Stop Bullying Task Force. You'll receive a certificate, T-shirt, ID card and membership into an exclusive website designed for Task Force Members only. There you will be able to interact with fellow Task Force members from across the globe to communicate your thoughts, suggestions and solutions to help others end bullying. There will also be activities and contests with amazing prizes.

---

[1] CDC
[2] National Youth Violence Prevention Resource Center

JOIN THE MOVEMENT TO **STOP** BULLYING

BULLIES BULLY KIDS WITH LOW SELF-ESTEEM

BULLIES ARE INSECURE

BULLIES ARE USUALLY BEING BULLIED

IF YOU'RE A BULLY *EVERYONE* KNOWS YOU HAVE LOW SELF-ESTEEM

BE TRUE TO YOU

HOW
TO USE
THIS BOOK

Step One

Read this handbook. You and your Task Force members will be asked **QUESTIONS** about bullying and its impact on a person's life. You will also be doing some cool exercises we've developed and others we've found. In each chapter and exercise **your team will need to email HeyUGLY@heyugly.org your answers, thoughts, suggestions and solutions**. You will know when to email us when you see a box that looks like this ...

From:	
To:	HeyUGLY@heyugly.org
Subject:	We will assign a subject line for you to use

Each time you send in your email we will send you an email to let your know that your answer have been added to your TASK FORCE FILE. Please be assured that your names and identities will be protected by Hey U G L Y and will not be used without your expressed, written permission.

Step Two

Get together with a group of friends and form your own **Hey U G L Y Stop Bullying Task Force**. Give yourselves a name. As an example, a Task Force from Michigan City, IN calls itself the St. Stans Stop Bullying Task Force. Here is your first task:

EMAIL your Task Force name to HeyUGLY@heyugly.org with **"Task Force Name"** in the subject line.

From:	
To:	HeyUGLY@heyugly.org
Subject:	Task Force Name

Step Three

When you and your Task Force complete all of the chapters and exercises in this handbook our Hey U G L Y Task Force Processing Team will enter you and your team as OFFICIAL MEMEBERS of **Hey U G L Y's Stop Bullying Task Force team.** You will receive a certificate, official T-shirt, and ID card. As an **OFFICAL STOP BULLYING TASK FORCE MEMBER** you will also receive a password for access into an exclusive website where you will be able to interact with fellow Task Force members from across the globe. There you will be able to communicate with each other on your initiatives, concerns and suggestions. There will also be surveys, activities and contests with amazing prizes.

Your suggestions and comments are important to us and we will be sharing them with students **THROUGHOUT THE WORLD**.

All of your answers will remain anonymous unless you specify otherwise.

Please send all correspondence to us at HeyUGLY@heyugly.org. If you don't have access to email you can send your answers and suggestions to:

Hey U G L Y, Inc.
PO Box 345
Rolling Prairie, IN 46371

Choose
TO
CHANGE

BRING
STUDENTS THAT
ARE **ALONE**
INTO **YOUR**
GROUP

BE
KIND

IF **YOU** SEE
SOMEONE
BEING BULLIED
HELP THEM
OUT.

BE
NICE TO THE
NEW KIDS
IN SCHOOL

CHAPTER ONE

WHY AND WHO DO BULLIES BULLY?

How many of you have been bullied?

Get together with your Task Force
and discuss the following:

- What kind of bullying have each of you encountered?

- How did being bullied make you feel?

- Were you bullied in private or was it in a group or public place?

- Would you forgive the bully if he/she were to apologize to you?

How many of you have bullied?

- Why do you think you bullied? 16-year old Violet said: "*A lot of the time, girls put each other down to make themselves feel better or because they're envious. I've made fun of people and talked about them because I secretly wish I had as much guts as them or a certain trait or talent.*"Teen Vogue

- Would you apologize to the person you bullied?

HEY U G L Y'S first Stop Bullying Task Force from **ST. STANISLAUS KOSTA SCHOOL** in the **U.S.** came up with the following reasons why bullies bully:

- *Bullies* are usually being bullied by someone

- *Bullies* feel insecure

- *Bullies* have low self-esteem

- *Bullies* have displaced anger

- *Bullies* feel left out

- *Bullies* suffer from peer pressure

- *Bullies* think it will help them get revenge

- *Bullies* are jealous

- *Bullies* are often depressed

- *Bullies* feel scared so they feel a need to hurt others with their words or action

QUESTIONS TO ANSWER:

QUESTION #!: Why do you think people bully? Email your answers to HeyUGLY@heyugly.org with **"Why do bullies bully"** in the subject line.

From:	
To:	HeyUGLY@heyugly.org
Subject:	Who do bullies bully

QUESTION #2: Would you forgive the bully if he/she apologized to you? If so, why? Email your answers to HeyUGLY@heyugly.org with **"Would you forgive a bully? If so why?"** in the subject line.

From:	
To:	HeyUGLY@heyugly.org
Subject:	Would you forgive a bully? If so why

CHAPTER TWO

WHO DO BULLIES BULLY?

NOW that you have uncovered why bullies bully, what type of person do you think bullies target and why?

Here is what Hey U G L Y's Stop Bulling Task Force came up with:

- *Bullies* bully kids with low self-esteem

- *Bullies* bully kids that are overweight

- *Bullies* bully kids that speak with a foreign accent

- *Bullies* bully kids with speech impediments

- *Bullies* bully minorities

YOUR SUGGESTIONS NEEDED: Can you add to this list? Email your additions to HeyUGLY@heyugly.org with **"Who do bullies bully"** in the subject line.

From:	
To:	HeyUGLY@heyugly.org
Subject:	Who do bullies bully

Hey U G L Y reports that the number one person the bully bullies is someone exhibiting low self-esteem. So, let's explore the physical aspects – body language - of the bully and the bullied. **Make a list** of the ways a person with **low** self-esteem appears outwardly. How do they walk, dress, etc.? **Make a list** of the ways a person with **low** self-esteem talks. Do they make good eye contact? Do they mumble? **Make a list** of the ways a person with **positive** self-esteem appears and talks. After you've made your lists take turns doing one minute skits as a person with low self-esteem and another skit as someone with high self-esteem. You may want to add these skits in your film for our *VIDEO CONTEST.* Videotape your skits and enter them in Hey U G L Y's *"BULLYING'S NOT COOL"* video contest. Go to *www.heyugly.org* and click on contests to get all the details and rules and regulations. The contest will be judged by filmmakers, some of whom have done films for MTV. *FIRST PRIZE IS A NEW VIDEO CAMERA.*

From:	
To:	HeyUGLY@heyugly.org
Subject:	How people w/low & high self-esteem act

Have you heard the saying, "Fake it till you make it? Wikipedia defines it as *"Imitating confidence so it will generate real confidence"* and cites an article from *Prevention* magazine where scientists asked a group of 50 students to act like extroverts for 15 minutes in a group discussion, even if they didn't feel like it. The more assertive and energetic the students acted, the happier they were.

> An extrovert is energized by being around others while an introvert is energized by being alone.

Since we determined that bullies go after people with low self-esteem please answer the following:

QUESTIONS TO ANSWER:

1. **Do you think** acting like you are confident will keep bullies from attacking you?

2. If so, **do you think** faking positive self-esteem can actually help you develop good self-esteem?

Discuss both of the above questions with your Task Force

ANSWER: Email your answers to HeyUGLY.org with **"Acting like you are confident"** in the subject line.

From:	
To:	HeyUGLY@heyugly.org
Subject:	Acting like you are confident

The same *Prevention* magazine article talked about a study which showed that "a law student's level of optimism in the first year of law school corresponded with his or her salary 10 years later. The impact wasn't measly: On a 5-point optimism scale, every 1-point increase in optimism translated into a $33,000 bump in annual income."

ARE YOU AN OPTIMIST??

An optimist is a person with a positive outlook on life. The opposite of optimist is a pessimist who habitually sees or anticipates the worst or is disposed to be gloomy. For example: Imagine you are waiting for a friend to meet you at a restaurant and he/she is not there at the time you agreed. A pessimist would worry that they were going to be stood up while the optimist would feel confident that the friend will show up.

If being optimistic could help someone make an extra $33,000 a year, how do you think it could help you in your life?

For the next couple of weeks be aware of how your mind works. Are you a pessimist or an optimist? If you discover you are a pessimist, would you like to **CHOOSE TO CHANGE** and become an optimist?

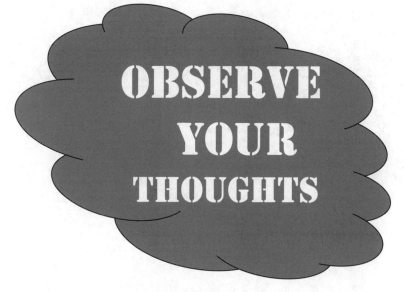

OBSERVE YOUR THOUGHTS

CHAPTER THREE

WAYS BULLIES BULLY

Now that you have uncovered the type of person bullies bully, what are the ways people bully?

Hey U G L Y's first **Stop Bullying Task Force** came up with the following:

- *Dirty names*

- *Name calling*

- *Pushing*

- *Fighting*

- *Spreading rumors and lies on the internet (cyber bullying)*

QUESTION: Ask your task force to add to this list and email us at HeyUGLY@heyugly.org with **"Ways bullies bully"** in the subject line.

From:	
To:	HeyUGLY@heyugly.org
Subject:	"Ways bullies bully"

CHAPTER FOUR

WHAT DO YOU DO IF YOU SEE BULLYING?

In our previous sessions your Task Force discussed why people bully. Do you remember everything on the list? Take a minute to review. You also discussed what type of people bullies target and did some role playing around that. You even discussed the ways people bully. Remember what you came up with? Take a minute to review.

Now discuss what you and your Task Force should do if you are being bullied. How can you help someone if you witness them being bullied.

Hey U G L Y's first Task Force came up with the following:

- If someone is bullying you ask them, **"Who is treating you so mean that you have to be mean to me."**

- If you are being bullied, and fear for your safety, immediately remove yourself from the situation and report your concerns to an adult you can trust like a parent, favorite teacher, principal or school counselor.

- If you are being cyber bullied don't keep it to yourself. Tell your parents, your teacher and school counselor.

> **QUESTION:** What would you recommend a student do if they are being bullied? Email your answers to us with **"What students should do if they are being bullied"** in the subject line.

From:	
To:	HeyUGLY@heyugly.org
Subject:	**What a student should do if they are being bullied**

REMEMBER: School staff is there to help you. More importantly they *WANT* to help! Most teachers are aware of the fact that bullies attack when they're not around so they hardly ever witness the incidents. Also, teachers need eye witnesses to come to your defense otherwise it's just **YOUR WORD AGAINST SOMEONE ELSE'S.** So try to get support from eye witnesses. Most importantly, if **YOU** see someone bullied **BE A WITNESS** FOR THEM!!!!!

AND – if you're worried about being labeled a snitch, DON'T BE. **YOU MIGHT BE SAVING SOMEONE'S LIFE.**

> **QUESTION:** What should you and your Task Force do if you see someone being bullied? Discuss this with your group and email HeyUGLY@heyugly.org your list of things to do. Put **"What we can do if we see someone being bullied"** in the subject line.

From:	
To:	HeyUGLY@heyugly.org
Subject:	What we can do if we see someone being bullied

Hey U G L Y's first Task Force came up with the following:

- If you are alone, walk over to the person being bullied and tell them you need their help to do something. Then take them away from the bully as calmly, but quickly as you can. Go to the principal's office and tell him/her what you saw.

- If you are in a group, form a circle around the person being bullied and tell them you want to hang out with them. Then get them away from the bully. Take them to a trusted adult and report what you saw.

TIME FOR ACTING AGAIN. Create a few STOP

BULLYING skits. They can be about **name calling, pushing, dirty looks, fighting, spreading rumors, etc.** Take turns being the teacher, the bully and the person being bullied. Remember to video tape your skits for entry into our **"BULLYING'S NOT COOL"** video contest.

TWO QUESTIONS:

1. How did it feel to be the bully?

2. How did it feel to be the bystander & a teacher?

Send your answers to both questions in one email to HeyUGLY@heyugly.org with **"How it felt to be the bully, teacher and bystander"** in the subject line.

From:	
To:	HeyUGLY@heyugly.org
Subject:	How it felt to be the bully, teacher and bystander

CHAPTER FIVE

CYBER

BULLYING

CYBERBULLYING
as defined by Whatis.com

The use of e-mail, instant messaging, chat rooms, pagers, cell phones, or other forms of technology to deliberately harass, threaten, or intimidate someone. Bullies can hide behind an electronic veil, disguising their true identity. This makes it difficult to trace the source, and encourages bullies to behave more aggressively than they might face-to-face.

Cyberbullying can include such acts as:

- making threats,
- sending provocative insults or racial or ethnic slurs,
- gay-bashing,
- attempting to infect the victim's computer with a virus, and flooding an e-mail inbox with nonsense messages.

If you are a victim, you can deal with cyber bullying to some extent by limiting computer connection time (not being always on), not responding to threatening or defamatory messages, and never opening email messages from people you do not recognize. You can also change you email addresses, change your Internet Service Provider, change you cell phone number, and attempt to trace the source of the bullying.

MAKE SURE YOU DON'T STRIKE BACK by responding because that behavior could lead to civil actions or criminal charges against you. Always tell your parents, teachers and the school counselor. In some cases, it may be advisable to inform the local police department.

QUESTION: Has anyone in your Task Force been cyberbullied? If so how did they handle it? We'd like to know. Email HeyUGLY@heyugly.org with **"How I handled cyberbullying"** in the subject line so we can pass your advice along to others.

From:	
To:	HeyUGLY@heyugly.org
Subject:	How I handled cyberbullying

The following pages contain a number of exercises designed to help you stay empowered instead of letting a bully get the best of you. Once you do the exercises **VOTE** on whether you think they can help other students around the world. Then email Hey U G L Y your verdict.

COOL

EXER-

CISES

I CAN SEE

Materials Needed
Paper, pens, pencils

EVERYONE stand and spread out so there's some space between you and the friends around you. Stand straight but relaxed, with your feet shoulder-width apart. Now raise your right arm and point the index finger of your hand straight at the wall in front of you.

Keep your feet in place and slowly begin to turn to your right, twisting at the waist. Go as far as you can and hold the spot. Look closely at the spot where your finger is pointing. Memorize that spot and slowly turn back toward the front.

Now lower your arm to your side, take a deep breath and relax.

Repeat the same procedures, but this time using only your mind.

1. Close your eyes and relax
2. Keep your arms at your side, do not move them
3. Picture yourself in your mind as you are standing
4. Picture yourself raising your right arm. Do not really raise it, just picture yourself doing so.
5. Imagine yourself pointing your index finger at the wall in front of you.
6. Use only your mind to picture yourself turning to the back of the room even farther than you did a few minutes ago. Picture yourself putting your hand back down to your side.
7. Turn back to the front of the room.
8. Open your eyes
9. Take a deep breath.

Now with your eyes **<u>open</u>** repeat this exercise again.

How many of your Task Force went further this time?

ISN'T IT AMAZING, that even though you went as far as you could the first time, this time you were able to go further? Many people find that they are able to go much further the third time they do this exercise. Why?

An important reason is that you *saw* yourself going further. Your mind has *tremendous* power over your body. Your body and mind are constantly communicating with each other. As your mind moves your body through this exercise, it tells your body that it can do more and your body then obeys. If an exercise that takes only a few moments to do has the power to make a change so quickly, imagine what you can accomplish with more practice. More important, **IMAGINE WHAT YOU CAN DO** as you turn your thoughts to things in your life that *really* matter. For example, if someone bullies you by calling you stupid and your mind keeps repeating *"I'm Stupid, I'm Stupid, I'm Stupid,"* do you think that will empower you? Of course not! But some of us still send ourselves negative messages. You'll learn how to cancel those out in our next exercise.

Michael Cortson, radio personality and author of the book, WINNING THINKING, often talks about the power of our thoughts and words. One of the things he asks his audiences is: **"IF SOMEONE CALLED YOU AN ELEPHANT WOULD YOU BECOME ONE?"** What do you think Mr. Cortson was trying to get his audience to understand?

Okay, so if calling you an elephant does not turn you into an elephant, remember, when someone calls you a negative name … **THAT IS NOT WHO YOU ARE.**

This visualization exercise can help you think differently. Instead of thinking *"I'm stupid, I'm stupid"* you can close your eyes and visualize yourself as smart. What if you study diligently for a test and then imagine yourself doing well on the test. Do you think that will

take some of the stress out of taking the test? Do you think it will help you to score better on the test?

I once read a report where they took a group of girls in one school and told them "girls always do badly on math tests." They went to another school and told a group of girls "girls always score high on math tests." What do you think the results were?

Here's the answer: Students who were told they would do poorly on the test did poorly while the students given the positive messages did better.

Have you ever walked into a party and felt that you weren't good enough or cool enough? Using this exercise of closing your eyes and thinking differently, what advice would you give to other teens and pre-teens to help them change those kinds of negative feelings?

VOTE:
1. Do you think this exercise should be a part of
Hey U G L Y's Stop Bullying Program for students around the world?
2. Please comment on this exercise. We'd like to know what you thought.

Email your vote and comment to HeyUGLY@heyugly.org with **"VOTE: Visualization Exercise"** in the subject line.

From:	
To:	HeyUGLY@heyugly.org
Subject:	Visualization Exercise

WHAT I LIKE ABOUT

On a blank sheet of paper write a title at the top of the page: *"What I like about _____"*

*On the blank line print **your** first and last name to finish the title.*

Exchange the paper with one of your friends. Make sure each friend has a sheet of paper with someone else's name at the top.

Now, write something that you like about the person whose name is on the top of the paper. It may be anything you like about them … something they do, the way that they treat people, etc. Keep it positive.

When everyone is finished writing something, pass the paper to another friend and repeat the exercise until all of your friends have had a chance to write something.

Take a few minutes and look at what has been written about **you** on your paper.

Look at the positive things others have said about **you**. Now take a moment and close your eyes to visualize yourself with those traits that were described on your paper.

FOUR QUESTIONS:

1. How does it feel to read these positive comments about yourself?
2. Did you find out any surprises about yourself that you were not aware of?
3. How do you feel about the surprises?
4. How do you think this exercise affects your self-esteem?

ANSWER the questions above and email them to HeyUGLY@heyugly.org with **"What I like about"** in the subject line.

From:	
To:	HeyUGLY@heyugly.org
Subject:	What I like about...

VISUALIZATION IS POWERFUL. In the Olympics they conduct something called "Visual Motor Rehearsal." They take Olympic athletes and hook them up to sophisticated bio-feedback machines. They ask the athletes to run their event only in their minds. Amazingly, the same muscles fired when they ran the race in their minds as the ones that fire when they run their race for real.

It's good to practice visualization every day. When you wake up, visualize how you want your day to go. Before a test, visualize how all of your studying will help you find the right answers. This will help you remain calm and focused. What are some other things you can visualize to help you go further in life? Have a discussion with your Task Force.

VOTE: 1. Do you think this activity should be a part of Hey U G L Y's Stop Bullying Program for students around the world? **2.** Please comment on this exercise. We'd like to know what you thought. Email HeyUGLY@heyugly.org your vote with **"VOTE: What I like about"** in the subject line.

From:	
To:	HeyUGLY@heyugly.org
Subject:	VOTE: What I like about

☑ **EACH MONTH** get together with your Task Force and discuss all the ways each of you used visualization help yourself. Give examples of whether it helped you in sports, on a test, interpersonal interaction, etc. We'd love to hear your success stories. Care to email us?

What is the "hue" of your skin?

Hue-Man Being Art Project™

Let's review the concept of *Hue-man Being*. The way it is being spelled for this exercise is **H U E M A N**. It is meant to remind us that we all have a lot in common as unique individuals on this planet. We are simply hued differently. To demonstrate the concept of *Hue-man Beings*, stand and form a circle. Now, roll up your sleeves and put your forearm next to the

forearms of your Task Force members. Notice how the hue of your skin is different than theirs.

Since the concept of *Hue-man Being* is that we all have a lot in common, have each Task Force member in the circle say something all human beings have in common. We've heard everything from all of us having eyes to everyone gets hungry. There are tons of things we have in common so have fun with this one.

Now that you've covered the **COMMON GROUND** of hue-mans, **LOOK AT THE DIFFERENCES.**

1. What does it mean to be different?

2. How do you define different?

3. What does it mean to you to be a different skin color?

4. Have you ever heard use a racially derogatory word? How did it make you feel to be around that?

NEGATIVE JUDGMENTS

It's time to examine how **NEGATIVE WORDS**, thoughts and actions can hurt ourselves and others. While you are still in the circle, have each person in your Task Force answer the following questions:

PART ONE

1. Have you ever been negatively judged?

2. Ask each Task Force member to share at least one example of something someone said to him/her that was negative.

3. Ask each Task Force member to talk about how it felt to be negatively judged. If you need help getting in touch with your feelings go to www.heyugly.org and click on the **"HOW R U FEELING"** link. Print out the list of feelings and see which ones fit the question.

4. Ask each Task Force member whose negative judgment/s really hurt them the most? Is it a family member? Friend? Teacher?

PART TWO

OKAY, IT'S TIME TO "FESS UP." Now it's time to talk about when **YOU** negatively judged others. You have just gotten in touch with how bad it feels to be bullied, it's now time to take responsibility for **INFLICTING THAT PAIN ON OTHERS!!!!!**

DISCUSSION

1. What were some of the negative things you said or thought about others? *Have each Task Force member recall at least one example.*

2. How did it feel to negatively judge someone else? *Make a list of your feelings. For example: Did you feel guilty? Afraid?*

3. Does peer pressure influence you to negatively judge others? Ask your Task Force to give examples of how peer pressure caused them to **BE MEAN TO SOMEONE**.

QUESTION: What were some of the examples your Task Force came up with regarding how peer pressure caused them to be mean to someone. Email the answers to HeyUGLY@heyugly.org with **"Why peer pressure can cause bullying"** in the subject line.

From:	
To:	HeyUGLY@heyugly.org
Subject:	Why peer pressure can cause bullying

PART THREE

*Have you ever negatively judged **YOURSELF?***

Have you ever stood in front of a mirror and called yourself stupid or ugly?

You know how bad a **NEGATIVE JUDGMENT AGAINST YOU** from another person feels. It's awful. Right? How does your negative self-judgment make you feel?

Each time you call yourself stupid, ugly, not good enough, etc., you are taking positive energy away from yourself.

OBSERVE YOUR THOUGHTS

Earlier in this exercise, we talked about the different types of people who judged us. Quite often the negative messages we give ourselves are not our own. Most of the negative judgments we have about ourselves come from somebody else ... a friend, family member, etc. It is human nature to actually believe the judgments of others and take them on as our own. It is our job to recognize that someone else's negative judgment of us is NOT WHO WE ARE. Has anyone ever called you a name and then you start calling yourself that name over and over and over? Discuss this with your Task Force.

DEFEND YOURSELF!!!

If a person called one of your friends "ugly" or "stupid" you would defend them, right? That's what you should do for yourself whenever you have a negative self-judgment.

How many times have you told your body that you hated it?

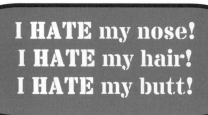

I HATE my nose!
I HATE my hair!
I HATE my butt!

Did you know **YOUR BODY HAS FEELINGS TOO**? Lots of time we treat our friends better than we treat ourselves. **THAT'S SO WRONG**! Award winning recording artist, **PINK,** was obsessing about her thighs until the day she visited children in a hospital and saw kids with no legs.

Our bodies help us all of the time. It is constantly there for us and we sometimes treat it worse than we would treat a stranger on the street. We call various parts mean names, we eat the wrong foods, we drink the wrong stuff … you know the drill. Take a few minutes and discuss this with your Task Force.

TWO ASSIGNMENTS:

1. Above we listed a few ways we treat our bodies badly. What are some of the other ways? Email us a list of 10 ways.

2. Make a list of 20 wonderful things your body does for you.

Email the lists to HeyUGLY@heyugly.org with **"I love my body"** in the subject line.

From:	
To:	HeyUGLY@heyugly.org
Subject:	I love my body

HOW TO CANCEL OUT ALL THE NEGATIVE JUDGMENTS

Take your index finger and press it to your thumb like you were squishing a piece of dirt between those fingers. Now, each time you make a negative judgment about others or yourself, press those fingers together and squish out that negativity. Immediately replace the negative judgment with a positive statement. Make a list of the things you like about yourself and concentrate on that.

RECALL A NEGATIVE JUDGMENT YOU HAD ABOUT YOURSELF and squish that negative thought between your fingers. Picture your inner-self and make a heartfelt apology to yourself then give your inner-self a compliment. How did you feel giving yourself a compliment?

The next time you have a negative judgment about yourself or someone else just **STOP**. Don't negatively judge yourself for having a negative judgment, just recognize it, squish it out and replace it with something positive.

To help keep other peoples' negative judgments and thoughts from affecting you, pretend you have a zipper on your body (like a zipper on a Hoodie).

 Now zip yourself up all the way to your mouth. Imagine you now have a protective shield around you that will not allow anyone's negative thoughts and judgments to penetrate. Pretend there is a lock at the top of the zipper. Give it a quick turn to lock in your protection. You may want to do this before you go into the mall. Where are some other places where zipping up your shield would be a good idea?

LOVE
YOURSELF

Call **your** voice mail and leave a message for yourself using whatever words you use to make a friend feel good when you leave messages on their voice mails. Make sure you end your message to you by telling you how much you love you. **IT WILL FEEL STRANGE AT FIRST**, but it will feel so good when you retrieve the message and listen to **YOU** telling **YOU** that **YOU** love **YOU**.

Experts say that you can't love someone else until you love yourself. They also say that if you want others to treat you well you need to first treat yourself well.

TREAT YOURSELF
BETTER THAN YOU TREAT
YOUR BEST FRIEND.

☑ **EACH MONTH** ask your Task Force how many times they were able to turn negative judgments into positives. Have them cite examples.

Go to http://heyugly.org and click on the Hue-Man Being Art Project link to see examples of artwork that have been submitted and read the rules and regulations.

In 2009 Hey U G L Y published a book of student artwork and put it on display in art centers. The book is called Hue-Man Kind, A Book to End Racism. Nick News sent a film crew from New York to Hey U G L Y's corporate office to film some of the students whose artwork made it into the book. The segment aired worldwide in February 2009.

Hue-Man Kind
A Book
To End Racism

50 Inspiring Works of Art
Created by Students
for Hey U G L Y's

HUE-MAN
BEING
ART
PROJECT™

by Betty Hoeffner

One hand one world
One body in all

Hey U G L Y will be collecting artwork from students 9 – 19 years old this year too. We will have art experts select the most representative works of art to be published in a new volume of our book.

WHY IS RACE THE FIRST THING WE SEE? IT SHOULD BE HOW BIG OUR HEART IS AND HOW MUCH WE HAVE TO CONTRIBUTE. WORLD PEACE IS AT OUR FINGERTIPS.

YOU DON'T HAVE TO BE PICASSO IN ORDER TO MAKE AN IMPACT.

STEP ONE

Draw a picture of **Hue**-*man Beings*, people of various hues, interacting in harmony on 8.5 x 11 white card stock. Feel free to use pencils, markers, crayons, or colored construction paper to create a work of art that shows **Hue**-man Beings connecting. It can be literal or symbolic. It can be stick people or whatever you want. (Go to heyugly.org for complete rules and regulations.)

STEP TWO

Somewhere **on** your artwork write two to three sentences about why it is important that we never judge a person negatively because of the color of his or her skin in order to end racism.

STEP THREE

On the back of your artwork write your:
1. Name and age
2. Address
3. Phone and email address
4. School

Annual Deadline is February 28.

NOTE: Go to http://www.youtube.com/watch?v=35uTLVmgN1Q to see a mini-documentary of the Hue-Man Being Art Project including the circle exercise

VOTE:
1. Do you think this exercise should be a part of Hey U G L Y's Stop Bullying Program for students around the world?
2. Please comment on this exercise. We'd like to know what you thought. Email your vote and comment to HeyUGLY@heyugly.org with **"VOTE: Hue-Man Being Art Project"** in the subject line.

From:	
To:	HeyUGLY@heyugly.org
Subject:	VOTE: Hue-Man Being Art Project

RIP YOU TO TEARS

Materials Needed: Sheet of white paper, sheet of construction paper (any color), glue or scotch tape.

FOR this activity have everyone in your Task Force draw a self-portrait. Make the picture cover as much as the paper as you can. Give everyone ten minutes to draw this picture.

Once the pictures are drawn select one Task Force member to begin the exercise. Ask this person to recall a negative name or bullying situation they have experienced and share it with the group.

When he/she finishes the story instruct everyone to rip their self-portraits two times. Continue this process of ripping the self-portrait twice after each Task Force member has shared their story.

At the end of this process all of the Task Force members should have the exact same number of rips in their artwork.

Instruct everyone to **PUT THEIR PICTURES BACK TOGETHER** using the construction paper as the base. Give the Task Force five minutes to complete this exercise. Most of your Task Force will not be able to put their self-portraits back together, which is appropriate for this exercise.

Start a discussion with your Task Force about what they think this exercise is supposed to help you realize.

Discuss how it felt to rip your picture after the Task Force members shared their stories with the group?

Discuss whether you think this exercise will help you think twice before saying something negative to someone?

Do you think it will help you stop sending yourself negative messages?

Make notes and report your findings by emailing us with "Rip you to tears" in the subject line.

VOTE: 1. Do you think this exercise should be a part of Hey U G L Y's Stop Bullying Program for students around the world?

2. Please comment on this exercise. We'd like to know what you thought.

Email your vote and comment to HeyUGLY@heyugly.org with **"VOTE: Rip you to tears"** in the subject line.

From:	
To:	HeyUGLY@heyugly.org
Subject:	VOTE: Rip you to tears

VISUALIZE THE YOU YOU WANT TO BE

CALL YOU TO TELL YOU THAT YOU LOVE YOU

IF I MADE IT THROUGH THIS I CAN MAKE IT THROUGH ANYTHING

SOMETIMES, no matter how hard you try, you will find yourself in difficult situations. Occasionally these circumstances may seem so bad that you do not know how you will be able to get through them. Today we will identify sources of strength inside of you that may help you survive these situations. In fact, once you get the hang of it, **YOU WILL FIND THAT TOUGH TIMES ARE ACTUALLY OPPORTUNITIES FOR YOU TO BECOME STRONGER**. If you know anyone who is having a tough time and you are worried about them check out our resource page at the back of this book for help center hot lines.

Have the Task Force members remember a situation in their lives when they feared they would not survive but did.

After each story ask the Task Force member if something positive actually occurred after they survived the tough situation. Did a break up with a boyfriend or girlfriend actually end up opening the door for a better relationship with someone else? Did a move to a new town end up helping them make better friends?

Award-winning recording artist, **Taylor Swift,** says, "However hard and painful they are, you will learn something from [a breakup]. That is the most contrived, you've-heard-it-a-million-times lesson, but I really do feel like everything is put in your life to teach you something-even if it's terrible and hard." GL Mag

On a piece of paper write across the top: **"IF I MADE IT THROUGH THIS**

I CAN MAKE IT THROUGH ANYTHING." Write down various situations that you thought you couldn't survive. Reflect upon those difficult times and write down the strengths that helped you overcome them. The next time you are in a situation and the pain is just too much, and you think you can't make it through, talk to a friend or trusted adult. Sometimes just talking about things helps so much. Often the people you share your situation with have been through what you are going through. They may be able to help you see sides of the situation that you can't see.

Try this visualization exercise to help you through the tough times.

VISUALIZATION EXERCISE

Remember, in as much detail as you can, those other times when you didn't think you were going to make it through a tough situation **BUT YOU DID**. Now, picture yourself making it through this new situation. See yourself looking back on your current situation just like you are looking back at a previous situation that has already been resolved. **REMEMBER THAT YOU ACTUALLY BENEFITTED FROM HAVING SURVIVED THOSE OTHER**

HARD TIMES and that you will most likely find rewards once you make it through this tough time. Remember to keep your eyes closed and breathe deeply as you visualize. Make yourself calm and relaxed.

Even when circumstances seem so bad and/or so different from what you experienced before, you will benefit from remembering that you have previously felt that sense of helplessness and fear. But just like rain gives way to sunshine those terrible feelings don't last forever and happiness will return.

Remembering the situations you made it through in the past is an indicator that you will be able to survive again in the future. Often it is necessary to outlast the situation and that endurance may be all it takes to get through.

When you are in the thick of a tough situation it is important to manage your stress. Following are two stress-reducing exercises that can help you.

#1 STRESS REDUCTION EXERCISE

CLOSE YOUR EYES and inhale <u>slowly</u> through your nose to a slow count of four —one, two, three, four. Now, exhale slowly through your mouth to the count of eight—one, two, three, four, five, six, seven, eight. Do this very slowly. Repeat this exercise 10 times making sure your eyes are closed. How does your body feel? Is it relaxed?

#2 STRESS REDUCTION EXERCISE

This is going to sound crazy but trust us; it really works to reduce your stress. Ask your Task Force to start laughing. Big, deep laughter. Have a contest to see who can laugh the longest nonstop. It's called Laughtercising™. When you finish notice how your body feels.

QUESTION: How did you feel after laughing so long? Would you use laughter to help reduce stress? Email your answers to HeyUGLY@heyugly.org with **"Laughing"** in the subject line.

It's been proven that laughter reduces stress and increases energy. It even can impact weight loss. According to TV fitness expert, Denise Austin, *"Laughing is great exercise. It tightens your abs, gets your endorphins going, and filters out all those anxieties that weigh you down."*[3]

---

[3] Redbook Magazine

Doctors recommend 15 minutes of laughter each day for optimum health and stress reduction. Hey U G L Y created a CD of contagious laughter specifically to help students de-stress. It's called "Laughtercising™". **WE MADE IT 60 MINUTES LONG SO YOU CAN ALSO PLAY IT QUIETLY AS BACKGROUND NOISE WHEN YOU'RE UNDER STRESS STUDYING FOR A TEST**. It will take your stressful frown and turn it into a smile.

VOTE:
1. Do you think the visualization exercise should be a part of Hey U G L Y's Stop Bullying Program for students around the world?

2. Please comment on this exercise and the stress reduction tips. We'd like to know what you thought.

Email your vote and comment to HeyUGLY@heyugly.org with **"VOTE: If I made it through this"** in the subject line.

From:	
To:	HeyUGLY@heyugly.org
Subject:	VOTE: If I made it through this

CONGRATULATIONS!!!

You have now completed the Stop Bullying Course which has earned you membership into Hey U G L Y's Stop Bullying Task Force. We will process your Task Force File and send out your official membership package.

The only thing left to do is to administer the stop bullying pledge to your Task Force. With your right hand raised, ask your Task Force to repeat the following pledge.

I PROMISE TO STOP BULLYING

A
N RESPECT
D OTHERS FEELINGS

YOU COULD WIN A $500 US SAVINGS BOND BY ENTERING OUR COOL CONTESTS

Hey U G L Y's Annual

ESSAY CONTEST

Take a stand against bullying
and help compete for

$500 US SAVINGS BOND

by entering Hey U G L Y's
annual essay contest.
Write an essay about why you think
having positive self-esteem
can stamp out bullying.

Find rules and regulations at
www.heyugly.org/contests.php. While you're there
check out Hey U G L Y's annual Acronym contest and
don't forget the Stop Bullying Video Contest.

DEAR MS. HOEFFNER,

THANK YOU SO MUCH FOR THE SAVINGS BOND, T
PLAQUE, T-SHIRT, AND THE NEWS ARTICLE. I AM HONORED
MY ESSAY WON IN THE HEY UGLY ESSAY CONTEST. IT MI
A GREAT DEAL TO ME. I LEARNED SO MANY THINGS IN WI
MY ESSAY - SUCH AS TO TREASURE MY OWN SELF-ESTEEM
TO HELP OTHERS SEE THE GOOD THINGS ABOUT THEMSELVES
I REALLY APPRECIATE ALL YOUR HARD WORK AND YOU'VE
IN FOUNDING THE HEY UGLY PROGRAM FOR KIDS JUST LIKE
YOU GIVE TODAY'S YOUTH A CHANCE TO GROW AND LIVE
THEIR POTENTIAL, AND I AM VERY GRATEFUL. THANK YOU,
MS. HOEFFNER.

SINCERELY

ALICIA MCDONALD

P.S. ENCLOSED IS PICTURE

Hey U G L Y's Annual

ACRONYM CONTEST

Turn a negative into a positive
and vie to win a

$500 US SAVINGS BOND

Simply come up with a positive acronym
for any, or all, of the following words:
Dork, Loser, Hate, Racism or Stupid

Find rules and regulations at www.heyugly.org/contests.php/
While you're there check out Hey U G L Y's annual Essay contest and
don't forget about the Stop Bullying Video Contest.

SPREAD THE
W   O   R   D

Now that you've completed Hey U G L Y's Stop Bullying Program, help others learn to get in touch with their "inner cool." Contact the local elementary schools in your area and secure permission to be a guest speaker in some of the classrooms.

Do you still know the principal at your grade school? Call him or her or stop in for a visit to discuss how you can help their students learn how to stop bullying.

Wouldn't you have loved to have had this program when you were younger?

Let us know what schools you will be contacting.
Email HeyUGLY@heyugly.org with **"Spread the Word"** in the subject line.

From:	
To:	HeyUGLY@heyugly.org
Subject:	Spread the Word

RESOURCES

Dating Violence Helpline for Teens	866-331-9474
Domestic Violence Hotline	800-799-7233
Family Violence Help Line	800/222-2000
National Youth Crisis Hotline	800-442-4673
Suicide Help Line 800-SUICIDE	800-784-2433
Trevor Suicide Help Line	866 488 73860
U.S. National Teen Dating Violence Helpline	866-331-9474
Youth America Hotline!	877-968-8454

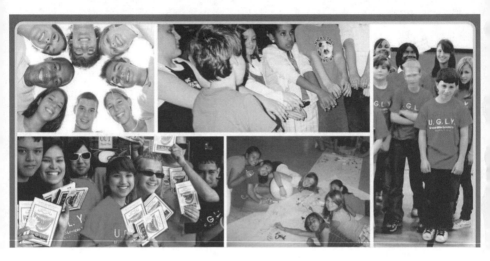

Thank you for doing your part to put an end to
bullying!